WEDNESDAY POETS

A Collection

Mole Hill Ink
South Reading, Vermont

ISBN: 978-0-578-68760-5

First Edition, 2020

Printed and bound by Ingram Content Group

Cover Art *Sheltering Tree* by Jill Herrick-Lee

Cover design by Wayne Thompson

Book design by Sarah Dickenson Snyder,
Brooke Herter James and Peter James

Mole Hill Ink

Molehillink@gmail.com
www.Molehillink.com
218 North Puckerbrush Road, South Reading, VT 05153

Proceeds from this book
are offered as a donation to the
North Universalist Chapel Society
of Woodstock, Vermont,
in thanks for inviting the Wednesday Poets
to meet in their library
for the past several years.

Guided by
Unitarian Universalist principles,
the North Chapel aspires to be
a congregation that nurtures
the growth and needs of its members,
sustains a strong spiritual life
within a loving church community,
and seeks to have a positive impact
on the world around us.

CONTENTS

Flowers, Fire—An Introduction

Rev. Dr. Leon L. Dunkley
North Universalist Chapel Society
Woodstock, Vermont

I'm learning to play a new song on the guitar. I am learning how to sing new lyrics. I think that the song that I am learning is a Wednesday song but it's hard to tell. I don't know for sure. What I do know is that the song that I'm learning belongs to thoughtfulness, reflection and intimacy. It belongs to an easy and uneventful, spring- or summer-time afternoon.

Poetry has times and seasons. Have you ever noticed that? It can be hard when times and seasons change…because the poetry changes as well and we do, too…right along with it. As time moves us away from autumn and winter, I am learning warmer songs again, new poetry. I am learning "Crow's Nest" by Kelly Joe Phelps. The first words are these:

> So, come along to the riverside
> Sit down now
> I just want to hear somebody else whine
> If you've got tomorrow, I've got a blade
> We can dig a hole into an old book
> Keep our secrets there

It's a great opening. Good poetry. I never thought about going down to the Ottauquechee with a good friend and a pocket knife to cut a hole and physically bury our secrets in an old book. What an image! What a great idea! I like words that lead to meaning that I did not know was there.

Poetry invites us into the nuances of life. It invites us into the nooks and the crannies of life, introducing us to the world in subtle and brand new ways. We grow our powers of discernment. We learn to appreciate fine detail. Poetry is like the ballet and the basketball of language—elegant and brutal, tender and competitive…just like us.

There are different kinds of poetry for the different seasons of the year and there are different kinds of poetry for the different times of day. In fact, of all of the early-morning poets, I think that the poet named Daybreak is my favorite. Her poems seem to have so little pretense. Daybreak writes,

> Silently, I steal upon the darkness
> No one ever sees
> The lovers were sleeping
> The fools were downcast
> The romantic prepare for the sunrise
> "Little darling…"

I love the poetry of Daybreak, even if she is the underdog.

Of all of the early-morning poets, I think that the poet named Sunrise gets most of the attention. He is so seductive. He is so masculine and triumphant…when he doesn't hide behind the clouds. On the good days, he sweeps us up in all things clear and bright and shiny. Sunrise deserves a lot of attention, to be sure. He does a lot of work. He carries the daily weight of possibility and inner potential. So, it is easy to see why he gets as much credit as he does. Sunrise is like the Robert Frost of early-morning poetry. Still, somehow, he is not my favorite. What can I say? I like the underdog. Daybreak is my favorite poet of the morning. And Wednesday is my favorite poet of the week. Obviously, because you are reading this, I am not the only one with a fondness for the Wednesday poets. What kind of poetry do we have in our hearts? What poems do we have in our community? The book that you are reading begins to answer these questions.

Poetry can be truly magical. It can be insightful and instructive. I think that we make a mistake when we assume that it is the job of a poem to be beautiful. A poem can be so many things…and that range of things is beautiful. In a poem called "A Dog, on His Master," poet Billy Collins writes,

As young as I look, I am growing older faster than he
Seven to one is the ratio they tend to say
Whatever the number,
I will pass him one day
And take the lead
The way I do on our walks in the woods
And if this ever manages to cross his mind,
It would be the sweetest shadow I have ever cast
On snow or grass

Billy Collins captures the bright-faith hope of Sunrise poetry—the vigor of youth, the rush of exploration on the wilderness path of life. Collins goes beyond this point. He also captures the deep-faith mystery of Daybreak poetry— the too-quickness of time, the sure-coming loneliness, the great limitations of our gifts to the world. Good poetry is a mix of things…just like us.

In the end, it hardly matters which one of the morning poets we admire most. They all have things to offer. We can learn from all of them. A poem is an opportunity to see the world in a different way. Whether we prefer the daybreak or the sunrise of the morning, whether we walk to the riverside and carve new secrets into an old book or whether we stay up late trying to learn a new song on the guitar, poetry invites us into something special.

So, here, we have book of poetry, a set of invitations to life itself. It is a book of bright-faith aspirations. It is a book of deep-faith inspirations. It is a book of poetry that changes in mood and season—just like us. Just as the inner life blossoms and the outer life is thrown to flame, poetry helps us to love this world more deeply, this ever changing world of flowers and fire.

PAMELA AHLEN

RED KAZOO

Gather every little thing—
angel wings and tulip shells,
black stones, white stones,
the purple feather laughing at your feet,
more purple than pickled beets.
Luxuriate in its beetness, its daffydility.
Place it next to the zebra key chain
and the rabbit's foot
in your cabinet of curios,
next to the Mai Kai matches,
the piece of driftwood shaped like Ohio,
the scribbled-on scrap: *Love You.*
Who are *You*? And who am *I*?
I'm a five-leaf clover, a damselfly,
a red kazoo tootling a zany song.
I'm the magpie behind that tree,
hunting the holy.

Pamela Ahlen

Beneath the paparazzi roaming Wilshire Boulevard
a saber-toothed cat lies mired in tar
beside the dire wolf and Pleistocene camel,
back when men wore more bristle than glitter—
not unlike today,
inhabited by more predators than prey.

I wander the exhibits of yellowed bones
and pollen grain, unearth the museum store trove
and buy a scarf of bled-down blue —
the sky today like the scarf,
smeared streaks draped above the black basin,
life imitating art imitating life,
the scarf a remembrance of past and future—
the last ice age, the next—another seep of bones,
female biped of a certain age,
fossil scarf around her neck.

In winter
I sometimes wake feeling like a moan
clouding the ground,
needing a place inside where joy might reside—
like entering a huge white space and
finding a thimbleful of red to affect my sanguinity.

Joy is the goal, isn't it?

"Why do two colors, put one next to the other
         sing?"—
something even Picasso had no word for,
something that can burn out winter blues,
like seeing the white mantle of morning
in all its tender ferocity,
seeing a redbird in snow.

WILD GINGER

Bloodroot pokes through winter's debris—
and mine—joining a gathering of upbeat blue
hyacinths bright as keeping myself shuttered
is dark, trillium unwilling to form a tidy red row,
a rebellion I secretly admire,
like defying rules of containment.
Bleeding hearts dangle like baubles from a bracelet:
every note never struck, relics of regrets—
but curatives, too, for new spring
fevering my core. No coincidence

I was born at the time of wild ginger,
curious brown thimbleful of flower
sized to hold a charm, a drop of rain.
Again I root under green fusion,
searching for its hiding place
cloistered in the fork of two heart-shaped leaves,
ready to unearth its beauty,
expose my own, blow our secret
to forget-me-nots who'll spring it on the woods—
those hidden away
have something singular to convey.

At the Color Me Beautiful party
women hold swatches under my chin—
a heat wave of pinks, yellows and jazz berry reds,
urge me to brighten my face. I confess to
yellow mania, admit I ate butter sticks like candy bars,
too young to understand the arterial ramifications,
glad every buttercup lit up my chin,
basking in yellow rays of amore.

But God's no buttercup,
and every other lover's yellow-bellied.
Any one of the four humors can go bad,
bile-yellow pestilence can turn a liver sick—
just a figurative skip from jaundice
to jealousy and fickle trickery.
Even Degas ranted about the horrors of yellow.
In spite of yellow sulphur mines, peevish lovers—
the nearest things to hell—

yellow's the color of canaries
and sweet-buttered corn, my sun-drops bikini.
Each spring I cook two quarts of dandelions,
add the sugar, a top note of golden raisins—
concoct a gold rush of chromatic wonder,
an Elixir of Mighty Restoration. I tell Degas
Van Gogh loved yellow, but he was crazy.

Pamela Ahlen

Lawn Party

Let the grass
shake loose its green
and blaze orange
with fire of hawkweed.
Let the grass
grow purple heal-all,
pink forget-me-nots and
wild celandine. Let the grass
hear the violets
sing the blues, the yowls
of the white pussy-toes,
the snap-clap toe-tap
johnny jump-ups.
Let the grass
drink the golden wine
of dandelion,
raise a holy buttercup ruckus.

PEGGY BRIGHTMAN

VIVALDI IN THE NY SUBWAY

In the infernal underground,
some separate women young and old
sit on the bench, wait for the next car.
Nearest us the dark-haired young man
cradles his cello, leans forward, lifts
the bow, begins the frantically
repeated,buzzing, cascading phrases...

Across the dark tracks
on the opposite platform, lit from
above, a windbreakered young man
stands at exactly the right moment,
grasps violin and bow, leans in
to join with the blooming, vibrating
pulsating counterpoint.

Together they spiral and rise
and rise, insist on carrying us higher
and higher, up and up and up to the gates
of paradise until finally the roar of the
approaching train supplies the
crescendo, the collapse of the
ending...apart yet together.

The battle-worn old men around us
are falling slowly—like aged trees
whose rain-soaked roots have given way.

Like shooting stars, their departure
leaves holes in our universe
we are unable to fill.

Music they made imprints our minds
mixing with the sound of sand
ebbing from the hourglass.

Stalwart, resolute warriors, knees
stiffened by resolve, one by one
they topple, fall into tall grass.

From our once proud banner,
stars have gone missing,
unstitched, worn, torn away.

Friends and heroes fall like leaves
into that glorious fall quilt of maples,
ash, sumac, promising to warm us.

The fourth horseman guides his pale horse
toward us, from the bend in the road,
bits and spurs jingling, hoofbeats mud-muffled.

Heard but unseen, his coming presses on us,
heavier than gravity; we huddle together inside,
clutch at each other, crumple to the floor in dread.

The fourth horseman waits for us nearby;
his horse stamps, breath rising in a cloud of steam.
Inside we press against the door.

Outside, all the charm of the world beckons—
the sunlight streams on the hemlocks,
the birds sing in the thickets; everything is waiting for us.

The rider is waiting for us to come out in grateful sunlight.
There he will embrace us; we will bow down, taste dirt
in our mouths, our falling will allow Mother Earth to
survive.

When the time comes, let me sleep. Isn't it enough
that all the atoms and molecules that danced
in the bodies of Plato, Botticelli, Attila the Hun

have been reborn in us? Reborn in the grass,
trees, in rain and ocean tides, in the cicada's
serenade to autumn? Nothing is lost.

Great nature recycles herself. Let me rise as ash,
fall as cinder,
drop deep in the waters of the Ottauquechee
flowing to the ocean. Let my atoms and molecules

swim in the flukes of the great whale, echo in the song
of the sandpiper skittering on the deserted beach,
caper with the sand flea in the dunes.

When dark waves, rising seas, claim our ordinary lives,
then millions of souls
of grass and trees, elephants, hawks and bees,
all will join in the whirlwind of earth's next transformation.

Earth Day Thanks
>   *—to Douglas Sands, my 8th grade science teacher*

Ill-shaven in his moth-eaten sweater,
he taught us well to see and love this world...
asked us to wander through the town,
searching ponds and side lots, bending down

close to notice earthworms, beetles,
asked us to collect frogs, to gather
samples of native and exotic leaves
stolen from hapless neighbors' shrubs and trees.

In his classroom, we planned visits to the moon,
while his giant tortoise slowly scraped
past our desks along linoleum floors,
pining for his distant Galapagos shores.

Hip-deep we followed him into wet marshes,
dug hillside fossils. One snowy April, seeking
pileated woodpeckers, up Mount Chocorua he led us;
we learned to coil boas like scarves around our necks.

We left warm living rooms at night
to stand out in the garden, swim the Milky Way,
find whirling Andromeda with naked eye,
plot by the north star a course to sail by.

His lessons return to me on rainy days,
when robin's call is summoning spring;
opening my ears and eyes I see
the blooming rhododendron fill with bees.

PANDEMIC TANGO

You're the hole in my stocking, you're the stone in my shoe—
you're the cream in my coffee, so baby, don't be blue...
Come dance with me our doomsday duet, there's no space
or time for regret...put a rose in my teeth
and let's break a sweat; embrace it all, trapped in
four walls. On stationary bikes we pedal in tandem
our rhythms are random—is this a hike, or a samba?

Sweetheart, togetherness is an art couples perfect over time
with heart, zest, good humor, and zoom
and—where possible—separate rooms.
You do my laundry; I butter your toast.
Take my hand, darling man—
we're in for the long haul—
this kitchen our dancehall.

We're joined together—it seems like forever
in holy quarantine; so grab me, baby, dip and fall—
let 'er rip, as we climb the walls;
tangle me knee-to-knee,
ankle to ankle
in our glittering, sweet and mean,
Argentine Quarantine Tango.

BLAIR BROOKS

A sculptor once told me that he sought to capture
in-between spaces,
not the branches or the trunks
not the solids or the dark shapes.
Rather the light defines -
where meaning lurks,
where connections are born,
where love's origins derive.
Maybe that is where joy hides,
where mystery abounds and curiosity swells.

The pauses.
The in-betweens.
Empty nothings.
I paid little attention to them, until now,
and had even less appreciation for them —
except as a time to recover.
Now, these spaces have deep, bright energy.
I want to explore their richness,
make up for lost time.

MARCHING ON

No guarantees.
Can't take out insurance to assure meaning.
Time is meaningless.
Moments aren't.

A look.
The warm sky.
A crisp morning.
A rush of love.
A surprise splash.
Something completed.
A memory shared.
Words said.
Pain felt, and eased.
Hope realized.
An idea understood.
A forgiveness.
Praise offered or received.

There are no guarantees.
Except time—it will march on.
Pay attention.
Don't miss the moments—even the tiny ones.

BARRED OWL

Late in the night
still dark
calling for a mate
who who who who
a lonely soulful sound
maybe hopeful
anticipating what may come.
It flows into the darkness
very much a part of the night air
rolling through the silence
then quiet again.
The *who who* slides inside me
resonating quietly
peaceful, soothing, almost caressing.
I am not alone;
someone else is awake
in this darkest hour
this loneliest hour
partners together.

A Single Wave

Over and over again,
the gentle breeze
pushes waves onto the shore.
Tonight lying in bed
I can hear individual waves speak—
each voice a rich, distinct sound
subtly different from the next.
I listen quietly, trying to understand
what each one has to say.

GORGEOUS THINGS
~inspired by Mary Oliver

Will they last forever this year?
Intricate designs of yellow
standing tall, calling out spring while
weathering rain, wind, and late snows.

Sunlight washes over them
interrupted by dancing clouds that
briefly fill the blue spaces above as
they rip across the spring sky.

Crocuses have come and gone.
Hyacinths and scilla poked their heads through
last year's leaves to say a passing hello.
Tulips are too timid to come forth, yet.

But this year the daffodils stay
blasting their yellow cheer.
They are here as the sun comes up,
and bid goodnight as the evening light fades.

We are blessed by their cheery color far longer than
we may deserve
reminding us moments shared with
gorgeous things can last,
but not forever.

 Blair Brooks

The half cup moon hangs suspended.
A sliver separates it from the ridge top trees below
that reach to soften its landing on the horizon.
It pauses with silver orange glow,
taking one last look over its nocturnal domain.

3 AM. All is quiet, inside and out.
The frigid air seeps through every invisible crack.
Curling up under the covers, I contemplate the cold,
I fight its penetration. I counterattack,
pulling blankets up around my neck.

I am susceptible to cold now,
I am susceptible to dark.
The moonlight provides a modicum of solace;
soon, starlight remains the only spark.
Darkness seeps into the house.

Cold and dark both threats as never before,
together they wind,
they hit the body's core,
they hit the mind,
they pierce the soul.

I hang suspended above my horizon,
uncertain how far below me it lies.
I roll over and gain strength and warmth from her
        lying next to me,
hoping to see, together, another and another sunrise.
The moon, more full, will grace the sky again tonight.

Gone Winter

Some gray slicks of ice live on
but we walk now on the brown
of last year's leaves
and over the knuckles of roots.

I will miss the tracks of the foxes passing,
closing my eyes to conjure the magic,
the better to see the ruffled ruby fur
fluffed and warm in the wind.

To open them again
and see the white torch
of the deer's tail
bounding over the field.

I will miss the stove
and its constant demands
the kneeling, the bending, the loading
and the warmth it shares.

Safe inside, imagining through the crystal panes
that pale eyes blink at me from the tree-line
then disappear into a barricade
of fallen sticks and branches.

I will miss the crunch of my own boot
sinking to where the hay was cut
marching like a marionette
up the hill to home.

REWILDING

My woods are wilding anew
from the days
of men and sheep
wire and thorn
and the constant burning.

It begins as it ended
with the trees
in slow procession
shading the new ferns
smothering the old stumps.

Tender bark and beechnut
slender shoots and leaves
food of the forest
a forest now full of prints
scat and murmurs.

Flat as the marshes are
and frozen
so that every forgotten twig
or spear of common rush
now breaks the level contour of the ice
to snag the skates.

Such uneven reckonings
and the falling down
long coats for padding
and cautious leaning
no twirling or dancing
arm in arm for safety's sake.

Hard work, with small fires
burning the brush bankside
and hot cider on a log.
Triumph just to have gotten
this far. Soon the river
will freeze deep enough
to tempt us to the sea.

The Piano Teacher

She was surprisingly strict
for someone who smiled so much
her hair always up
suspended by chaos and pins.

She wore lots of makeup
not of the cheap variety
but more like an artist
might wear on a night out.

She listened with her eyes closed
ankles crossed below her dress
her hands miming the proper position;
through an open window…gardenias.

She sat stiff and upright, that's for sure
this was a job after all.
I felt her wince—
I don't blame her really.

A GIFT

I went into the field
and picked out something blue
in the far soggy corner
where the hay peters out.

It looked like a thistle
with a bonny blue knob
stinging the tips of my fingers.

I took it to the room
with the big heavy books
and pressed it there
between the beginning and the end.

So if my granddaughter someday
could read halfway through
the History of Everything
she would find it.

FALL AGAIN

Early reds and yellows
enter the young maples
knifing into late summer
already wheezing
from the last dust.

Windows close
freezers fill
one-tons deliver wood
busy are the saws and splitters.

Finches hear the click
and go.
Owls stay to mate
and fluff the snow.

Long lists and short days
burls turn to bowls
in nice warm sheds
webs fray in the
drafts of heat.

Rain hardens to sleet
blankets emerge
from the top shelf
and release the cedar
of their sleep.

It *is* a time of turning
rehearsed by all the gods
who must marvel
at all the things we put away.

The Offering

These woods
on the edges of a lake
are settling now
to winter darkness.
Whatever was going to die
is gone—
crickets, ferns, swampgrass.
Bare earth fills long spaces of a field.
But look:
a single oak leaf
brown and shining
like a leather purse.
See what it so delicately offers
lying upturned on the path.
See how it reflects in its opened palm
a cup of deep, unending sky.

An Ordinary Sunday

On Sunday, I sing in a church choir, not believing
in God, but holding a space for something—

some might call it spirit, an opening,
a candle illuminating a cave.

On Sunday, I climb the hill behind our house,
as the long winter thaws, and my dogs dig in wet loam.

I wait for worries to relax their hold, for my mind
to become one with the clouds' calm drifting,

the trilling of a stream rushing somewhere unseen.
We need, I think, to let ourselves soften around hurt,

before we melt, like spring snow, into fields—
so, I let Dad in, decades past his death,

find a few good memories, like stones just soft enough
for polishing—him filling the green glass vaporizer nightly,

so I wouldn't get sick, in the hot, dry air of my childhood
        winters;
Dad donning an apron to cook for his skinny teen.

I breathe in the care and nourishment he offered then,
and I receive today, on an ordinary Sunday.

OCTUBRE

If you saw me driving in this pelting rain,
you'd never guess my errand—
to buy lilies
for my butterfly.
He'll savor the aroma of flowers,
this cold November day,
since wild blooms have faded
into memory—if he has one.
Octubre lives in a screened-in cage,
because I couldn't let him out
in last week's snow, could I?
He seems content, his feet sticky
against the screen, pleased to drink,
when I uncurl his proboscis
with a toothpick, dip it
in honey water, while he sucks
through his trunk-like tongue.
I say *he* because he has two spots
like eyes, on his hind side,
that indicate *boy*—
good for our family
of two lesbians, two bitches
(a Shepherd and a Lab),
and thirty thousand girl bees
who spent the whole autumn
dragging the hairy drones
out of the hive, killing them,
dumping the corpses
in a heap out front.
I'm just saying, it's good to have
some masculine energy round here,
even if it's just one Monarch
who hangs upside-down all day
and sometimes flutters his gorgeous wings.

Laura Foley

I.
We moved the bed
so the head faces north,
a wisdom we read,
from India.
We dislodged a ghost,
her husband,
who on these sheets
three years ago expired.
We altered the angle
of our repose
and sleep all night
at peace, entwined.
We wake to morning hills,
trees, a great expanse,
a gentle, dappled light,
new to us.

II.
The patient avoids the hospital window's view,
turning from snow's glare and stripped
winter trees, focusing on photos of dogs,
children, his hunting awards taped to the wall,
all invoking home, where he'd prefer to be,
this large man, with his bright white beard,
who doesn't read much, doesn't pray—
except now, with me, both of us shy,
until his eyes tear—
and his body shines from inside.

III.
No dappling leaves,
but enough snow
on near branches now
to illuminate our window,
winter light grown greater
with snow's reflection.

IV.
We begin it with experiment,
hurling boiling water
to the frozen air,
watching it glitter
like glass confetti
crackling in the new year—
an answered wish
in every shining shard.

V.
Cold wind whips snow
so it swirls around our tallest pine,
a halo of light circling
a frigid angel or ghost
from my or someone else's past
seeking company,
or just floating in the crisp winter air
for the wonder of it.

VI.
Not brown, not rust, but inexplicably white as bones,
these remnants dry as dust recall life, crackling,
as wind shivers them in barren early spring—
not one bud yet gracing it,
white leaves clung through snow and ice,
to shine and tremble in this Sunday light.

     Laura Foley

VII.
The dog shivers,
wet from a late spring swim,
whimpers as the wind
pulls light from the pond,
and we sit in shadows,
by the water she knows,
just last summer, shone gold.

VIII.
This sip of coffee
over so quickly,
this guiding lighthouse
in the mist-less harbor,
moments before
the season changes,
this slip of wind along the bay,
a sweater saving me from chill,
this precious slant of summer sun,
clouds arriving to veil the light,
a gentle voice of waves on stone,
It's this, it's this, it's this.

IX.
I walk this foggy dawn to see the seals
where they sleep beneath the scrim
rain makes of rising light,
to hear the music of their steady breath—
a holy time before the changing of the tide.

DEBBY FRANZONI

CASHING IN ON HOME SCHOOLING

Today on my walk
I met a grandfather and his grandson
at the culvert bridge.

The man had a rake,
tugged at the weeds growing
over a grate, pushed logs away,

asked the boy
if he remembered
that beavers eat cambium

not bark,
…asked,
"Does the cambium deliver nutrients?"

The seven-year-old said, "No, it's for growth."
A fisherman not far away chimed in,
"The xylem and phloem carry."

"The xylem delivers food to the leaves,
the phloem returns it to the roots,"
the boy yelled past me to him.

I left them naming the pines in Latin
as I whispered, zylum, phone-um, cambreum,
over and over, all the way home

so I wouldn't forget. I wanted
to look the words up
so the next time I saw

new piles of branches and logs
strewn this way and that along my path,
I'd know more about them.

Debby Franzoni

I'VE ALWAYS WONDERED WHY PEOPLE FISH

So today I sit at the end of the dock
let my feet dangle in the water
watch a man in a boat in the bay
cast his line into a pin-prick portal of entry.
After a catch he sits, his boat rocking,
his pole wedged between elbow and ribs,
adjusts his blue canvas hat to shield the sun
and directly beneath his nose he wraps
a worm around the hook, then with a flick
of the wrist he casts the line away.
We sit and wait. Soon he stands
to reel in silver strands of lightning leaping
out of the water. The fish arches and argues
its case to the side of the boat. The man leans
over the gunnel, grabs the catch, frees it
from the hook, drops it into a pail at his feet.
Then he hugs the pole to his side,
takes another worm….
I watch until his every move is mine,
and the wide lake, the near island,
its pines that reflect full length
in the silent water and the cotton ball clouds
that coast in the blue sky over our heads.

BARBED WIRE

Just last week I learned
my friend is related
to the man who invented
barbed wire which is why
I pause in a poem I am reading
about the night a boy and his father
on their way to fish cross the rusted strands
of a barbed wire fence in the moonlight.

I've read stories like it before—
a boy and his father out together
lassoing a wild horse
in the moonlight, but I don't know
who invented the lasso
so I wouldn't stop to wonder
that it was even invented
or the boots they wore,
invented by someone,

the two agreeably smiling,
talking now and then,
knitting their bond together
in language, though sparse, invented,
even the rules for its punctuation, invented,
the inventors invisible,
so I never stop to think about them
or their inventions—
not even the moonlight.

 Debby Franzoni

Running on Empty—Quarantine Day Forty

My favorite diner's
  CLOSED sign

has lost
  its "S".

This morning I sit here quiet,
  with the cat on my lap.

I have one hand poised
  on its soft, allergen back.

Like in a painting
  hung at the Louvre,

a portrait of a woman
  with intelligence.

My great still eyes
  stare out the window

toward the morning
  sun and

I have
  a slight smile.

But underneath I harbor
  ordinary notions,

like a deep desire
  for a cup of coffee

at the Sunrise Diner,
  the one that's CLO ED.

Debby Franzoni   50

TRAPPED

Every morning I get up
check the weather
with a look out the window,
listen to the birds
up hours before me.

I make a cup of coffee
watch the water flow into my cup
with the joy of crushed coffee beans
harvested so far away I cannot
imagine the trip they made

to get here and the pleasure
they feel now
released from the box,
their gratitude, an aroma,
mingling with new air

escaping into a new place
checking out this reality
and its different ways
from living in a box.
For me, its release,

a diversion from living
in my self-imposed
four-walled box
waiting for someone
bigger than I to let me go

Debby Franzoni

so I, too, can wake up in a new place,
even if it's here where I imagine
I will mingle differently than I did,
for time passes without us,

so in my heart I know
what was left behind
did not wait. It's gone.
What I will embrace
is a new angel, also with dreams.

JILL HERRICK-LEE

Land to Tend

Startled—
birds fly

sky-ward
hover over nests

in a distant
helpless tending—

They aim to land
when threats cease—

I did not see myself
in this way—

when I disturbed them
with my shovel and my groans—

I did not notice—

such important work

Heavenly Blue reminder—

You reach and rise
in spirals
counterclockwise

as if you understood
or could measure time—

flower by flower
flung open
to trumpet each offering of light

Stargazer (*Lilium orientalis*)

What unseen lover
coaxes you
to open up
so unabashedly red
to tip your sultry head
heavenward

It's enviable
the way you unfurl yourself
for this day
and into the night

Across the moonlit yard
your musky scent
drifts
like a lover's cry
through summer windows

HELIOPSIS
...striking and colorful...this stunner doesn't know how to quit blooming.
        —Sugar Creek garden catalogue

I planted this
fierce
yellow flower

My daughter
colors
her hair blonde

then red
blazes
through summer

She tries something new
for fall
A punk hairdo

in my garden
Spiky stalks
startle me

where tiny fingertips
once revealed
the first gentle indication

of something taking hold
My child
this wild profusion

bursting open
She marches forward
determined as any

well rooted flower
to stand her ground
to show me how to bloom

ONION

Circles moving outward

from the center

the weight of a stone

thrown into water—

for now—my love—

the onion is full of tears

It needs you to cry them

To forget is not to forget

but to lay it down for a while

to lay it down again—

I rest by the river

water washes over stone

shadows land at my feet

In the reflection

the deepest blue window of sky

opens up like a cathedral

through the highest branches

Above and beyond

the world is full

of sunlight and dove song

To arrive in any moment

is to arrive restored

to forget is not to forget

HOT DOG

I'm gonna bite you. Hard.
And when I do
I'll be coasting down Comm Ave
on my rusty red Raleigh,
dragging a faded blue sneaker
just in case the brakes don't work.
I'm gonna bite you,
and when I do
I'll hear my mother say
Don't ruin that shirt
as a big blob of mustard
follows the ketchup onto my jeans.
I'm gonna bite you,
and when I do
I'll be watching Big Papi hit a homer
under the lights at Fenway,
or bench-sitting in the Garden,
or riding the café car somewhere
between South Boston and NYC,
looking out a grimy window
at the dazzling sea.
I'm gonna eat you in three chomps
and wish for a fourth.
I'm gonna bite you
and every time I do
I'm gonna be happy.

     Brooke Herter James

SOUTHBOUND, MAINE TURNPIKE, LABOR DAY

Give me big black crows on the Route 95 median strip
and I will give you twelve years old lining the cracked
back seat armrest of our station wagon with the
peppermints I've licked out of my HoJo's ice cream
cone staring out the open window on the long hot tar
drive home from summer listening to my parents
natter thinking about what I will wear to the first day
of school if there's any mail waiting for me if my room
will smell like late August grape jelly if my fish tank
will be slime green if a boy with a lisp will stand
under the street light tonight and call out my name.

Give me big black crows on the Route 95 median strip
and I will give you sixteen and three quarters still
sucking on peppermint bits thinking about the first
day of school where my locker will be who's in my
homeroom begging my mother to turn the radio dial
my father to drive faster so I can take the car to the
mall navigating 287 or the Saw Mill windows down
diet coke between my legs the boy with the lisp
replaced by the boy whose musty wool scarf I keep
under my pillow.

Give me big black crows on the Route 95 median strip
one year later and I will give you my father living
somewhere else my sister too now my mother driving
so slowly hands eleven and one cigarette burning
wanting to play the license plate game me sitting in
the front seat bare feet on the dashboard hating the
taste of the words in my head wishing for something
I can't name.

SUN DOG, WOLF MOON
12/31/2016

We woke to a Sun Dog
splitting the sky,
three suns out of one,

a halo of light enshrouding
the sugar maple at the edge
of the snowy drive.

Must be the cold, we said.
I had seen cold work its magic before.
Diamond dust in the Gallatin Valley.

But this was something else.
Later we returned from evening chores,
the donkeys fed and watered,

our breaths shortened
by the crystalline freeze.
Behind us a Wolf Moon rose

silent and huge over the barn
to the east, throwing our shadows
down long before us,

as if to say *stay awake*.

Spring Took the Long Way Around

this year, a shy schoolgirl
lingering along field's edge
as the boisterous ones
gather their sleds, hang skates
off hockey sticks, suck snow
from soggy wool mittens
and wander off.
They stayed too long —
they know it, but the ice
was so black and smooth.
They call over their shoulders
at the girl hesitating
by the stone wall,
We're done here, it's all yours.
She waits to be sure
they are gone for good.
Then holding her skirts high
above soft snow she ambles
across the pasture.
This is mine now she thinks
as she breathes her warm breath
such that the maples blush red
at their tips and the last ice
melts from the pond.

WHILE I WAIT

At the sidewalk café
a white-haired man
asks for coffee, hot,
cream, no sugar.

His daughter touches his sleeve
and points — the cranberry scones
in the glass case —
your favorite, remember?

His granddaughter splashes
in the ceramic dog bowl
brimming with cool water
on the porch step

where I sit shielding my eyes
from the sun with a menu,
the salmon pink impatiens
in the clay pots tremble

when a concrete mixer rumbles by,
spinning its vanilla and orange-striped drum.
Look, I whisper to the little girl,
a swirled ice cream cone on wheels.

Late August drifts by,
settles on my sun-warmed knees.
A friend of mine died
last week, I say to no one

as I wait for you to cross the street,
waving as you come.

Rolling up miles
of blacktop river
through chickpea
farms, feed lots,
slaughterhouses,
the Mississippi behind,
the Yellowstone ahead.
In between, the promise
of Wall Drug, cheap
gas, U-pick strawberries,
tattoo removals, corn
dogs, porn shops and
life without crystal meth.
Jesus everywhere, crackling
on the AM/FM/XM dials,
peeling off billboards,
smiling up from truck stop
placemats, coffee stain halos
and all. Checking out
of the Comfort Inn
to the pink of early sky,

I smell rain.

Wendy Ann Smith

Blue sky today, oh can't wait!
She gets up for breakfast, then
outside-leaps into the sunshine.
Aurora, Puerto Rican rescue pup is so
happy to bask in a warm Vermont day.

She bounds up the hillside,
first smells, then sees a
definitive fresh turkey track:
three toes forward, one small claw back.
The imprint is dominant and clear.

She spends most of her day indoors;
resting on her sofa-back window perch.
There Aurora can see the occasional bird.
Sometimes the turkeys are exploring
her driveway foraging for food.

The turkeys? Recovering from
near extinction fifty years ago; turkeys became
nearly nonexistent, gone for a century.
Importing revival wild turkeys became vital
as was Aurora's Vermont venture voyage.
Both now — striding about resplendently.

     Wendy Ann Smith

Two neighboring birch trees
in a meditation room's view,
their bases accented by a snow bank,
rise within steps of each other.
One top bends at ten degrees,
the other tree gracefully arches,
top branches reach and meet
framing their engaging portal.

ACADIA

Clear cloudless skies,
Precipice Cliff
peregrines' home.

Hurtling in, a bald eagle
sweeps towards their
nesting site.

Directly overhead
mother arches an
aerial defense.

Clashing birds,
inversions,
tangling talons.

Peregrines are the fastest bird.
Outmatched flying seaward, eagle.
Clear cloudless skies.

EIDERS

Oh, I so love common eiders.
Meditating this morning
what I espy are memories
from last week's trip. I see the
sand bask under sunlight at
Pebble Beach, while beyond
drakes bob about in Sandy Bay.
They sport a black skull cap with mask.
The rest of their body: an Oreo of black
belly and wings with white back and face.

The fashionably plumaged mingle
with reddish brown hen friends in
an assembled group called a raft.
Their eider feathers are a fine soft down
gathered for quilts from their nest linings.
The sparkling serene ocean is their stage
as they dive for mollusks in harmony.
This silent symphony blossoms
as my meditation metaphor, a vision
that flowers into my beloved Mom's song.

March

Orion's belt seen
through spring's soon to bud branches,
lights in the darkness

Sun's glow melts
May's morning new snow
creating a sparkling grass dew show.

SARAH DICKENSON SNYDER

Now A Hospice Volunteer

How shocked
I was as a child to learn
that the architecture
of life included death—
a frightened fire starting
inside of me fueled
by containment.

I have watched people die,
held their cool hands
as they exhale
a last breath.

Each time is a lessening,
an echo—the way veins
of a fallen leaf
are a faint imprint
of the tree or the inside whorl
of a shell holds onto the sea.

DAYBREAK

Muscling in the blinds
in lines of light,

the sun sharpens
your shoulder blades

as you sleep. I wake
with banners of words pulled

through a sea-side sky,
lift the covers' wide wing.

There is no quiet like morning,
no center flowering

like a journal opening.
I feel another symmetry

when I surrender
to the small gods

that pull my hand
across the page.

Over the aches of a planet
we are but a dusty second,

a shadowy group of foundations
just below the crust, easily sloughed.

This sculpture—our touch
might wear down the surface

the way marble steps remember use
by smooth indentation. In the busy halls

of entanglements, we are the flies
a trunk or tail swats away—

it'll move on, splashing river water
over itself, flushing the irritants,

swaying its immensity
through the catalogue of green.

     Sarah Dickenson Snyder

ON LEAVING

I will miss
even cleaning
the lint screen
each time I do
laundry, feeling
the mesh on my fingertips—
doing something I know
will lengthen the life
of a machine.

It starts with a shell—
its curve and shine,

the way a line peaks.
It starts with a star

and the arc
between bone and light.

An angled story
never ending—

a book blooming,
the gnarled woody parts

peeled to reveal the tender.
So much hardens

from the outside—
the denominator

of rain and sun
and unseen roots.

 Sarah Dickenson Snyder

Thats What It Is

As if there was some treasure
map handed to us as we left
the womb. Find *this*—a big X
at the intersection
of want and need.

Is that what pandemic means—
to be squeezed into silence.

Remember that nine months
we had to conjure ourselves?
And now a return—
a swimming in quiet.

My name is breath.

Even in my tears
there is inhale
and exhale.
We are always
rising and falling.

PAMELA AHLEN is program coordinator for Bookstock Literary Festival held each summer in Woodstock, Vermont. She organizes literary events for Osher (Lifelong Education at Dartmouth) and compiled and edited Osher's *Anthology of Poets and Writers: Celebrating Twenty-Five Years at Dartmouth.* Pam received an MFA from Vermont College of Fine Arts and is the author of the chapbook *Gather Every Little Thing* (Finishing Line Press).

PEGGY BRIGHTMAN first studied poetry in the 80's with Harold Bond at the Cambridge Adult Education Center. After a long modern dance career, she moved to Vermont and rediscovered poetry. Choreographing for her Moving Spirit Dancers, Peg creates unique poetry and dance events, such as the BOOKSTOCK 2019 *Tribute to Mary Oliver.* Publications include PoemTown Vermont (Poultney, Randolph, St. Johnsbury), and *Poets Reading the News.* She is a founding member of the Wednesday Poets.

BLAIR BROOKS (1953-2019) was one of the original three who met at a workshop at the Writer's Center in White River and moved to Woodstock to begin the Wednesday Poets. He discovered his love for writing poetry after he retired from his job as an internal medical physician at Dartmouth Hitchcock in Hanover, NH, due to a diagnosis of multiple myeloma. His poems teach, through his intense awareness of the moment, how to awaken what was always there within us. His wise, kind spirit remains at the heart and soul of our group. His book, *The Spaces In Between,* was published posthumously in 2019. His work also appeared in JAMA (Journal of the American Medical Association), in Telling Our Stories Through Word and Image (DHMC), as well as PoemTown Vermont.

J ON E SCHER spent thirty years working in Silicon Valley. He recently realized a long-held dream and retired to New Hampshire where he lives on a farm with his wife, daughter, and three dogs. He is the author of the chapbook *Here and There, Poems of New Hampshire and California (2017)*. When he isn't writing poetry, Jon tends to the farm and walks up and down the hills of New Hampshire and Vermont.

L AURA F OLEY is the author of seven poetry collections. *Why I Never Finished My Dissertation* received a starred Kirkus Review, was among their top poetry books of 2019, and won Honorable Mention in the Eric Hoffer award. Her collection *It's This* is forthcoming from Salmon Press in 2021. Her poems have won numerous awards and national recognition—read by Garrison Keillor on *Prairie Home Companion* and *The Writers Almanac*. A Hospice volunteer, Laura lives with her wife Clara Gimenez and their two dogs, among the hills of Pomfret, Vermont. www.laurafoley.net

D EBBY F RANZONI has always written poetry but began to write it seriously when she retired from teaching twelve years ago. Over the past several years, selected poems have appeared in PoemTown Vermont as well as in a six poet anthology, *Perhaps It Was the Pie* (2014). She is very appreciative for the generous help given to her by the Upper Valley, Woodstock and Castleton writers. She lives with her husband and two cats on Lake Bomoseen.

Jill Herrick-Lee is a poet and a visual artist. As a child, she developed a deep appreciation for nature exploring the wooded lakeside neighborhood she grew up in on the North Shore of Massachusetts. Jill's art has been shown in MA and VT. Her poetry has appeared in various collections, including *The Endicott Review* and *Zingology*. She is the mother of two grown daughters and "Gaga" to five grandchildren. Jill moved to the Upper Valley two years ago where she lives with her husband Michael on the edge of a forest in a mobile home they call The Happy Camper.

Brooke Herter James is the author of two poetry chapbooks, *The Widest Eye* (2016) and *Spring took the Long Way Around* (2019) and one children's book, *Why Did the Farmer Cross the Road?* (2017) Her poems have appeared in PoemTown Vermont as well as the online publications Poets Reading the News, New Verse News and Writing in a Woman's Voice. She was chosen as a finalist in the Poetry Society of Vermont's 2019 National Poetry Contest. She lives on small farm (lovingly referred to as Mole Hill) with her husband, four hens, two donkeys and a dog.

Wendy Ann Smith received her bachelor's degree in English from Plymouth State College where she was editor of the college paper, *The Clock*. She taught respiratory therapy at River Valley Community College for 28 years. In retirement her vision of returning to creative writing found a place and structure in this poetry group. That home has become her safe harbor for creating and enjoying the written word.

SARAH DICKENSON SNYDER has three poetry collections, *The Human Contract (2017), Notes from a Nomad* (nominated for the Massachusetts Book Awards 2018), and *With a Polaroid Camera* (2019). Recently, poems appeared in *Rattle, The Sewanee Review,* and *RHINO*. One poem was selected by Mass Poetry to be stenciled on the sidewalk for their festival, another nominated for Best of Net 2017. A hospice volunteer, she spends as much time as possible outside in Vermont. sarahdickensonsnyder.com.

ACKNOWLEDGEMENTS

With gratitude to the journals, collections, and contests that first published the following poems:

Pamela Ahlen's work:
Blue Heron Review: "Wild Ginger"
Cider Press Review: "Red Kazoo"
Comstock Review: "Elixir"
Finishing Line Press: "La Brea Tar Pits"
The Poeming Pigeon: "Lawn Party"
Postcard Poems and Prose: "Seasonal Affective Disorder"

Laura Foley's work:
Gemini Magazine: "Octubre"
Syringa (Star Meadow Press): "The Offering"
Valparaiso Poetry Review: "An Ordinary Sunday"
The Joe Gouveia Outermost Poetry Contest Grand Prize, judged by Marge Piercy: "Nine Ways of Looking at Light"

Brooke Herter James's work:
Spring Took the Long Way Around (Antrim House Press): "Southbound," "Spring Took the Long Way Around," "Sun Dog," "Wolf Moon," & "Heading West"
The Wildest Eye (Antrim House Press): "Hot Dog"

Sarah Dickenson Snyder's work:
300 Days of Sun: "The History of Mathematics"
Lily Poetry Review: "Daybreak"
One Sentence Poems: "On Leaving"
SWWIM: "Now A Hospice Volunteer"
Wax Poetry and Art—45 Poems of Protest: The Pandemic: "That's What It Is"
What Rough Beast: "The Elephant of the Earth"